Welcome from the Dean

Welcome to Lichfield Cathedral, the only medieval cathedral in England with three spires, known as 'The Ladies of the Vale'.

Today's sandstone cathedral, built over 800 years ago, is of a size to which human beings can easily relate. It is a spiritually warm place with a strong congregational life. We welcome you as a visitor or pilgrim to the shrine of St Chad, who brought Christianity to Mercia, and in whose honour the first cathedral was built in AD 700.

We hope you will be inspired by this beautiful building; that you remember it as a place where you found peace and refreshment; and that you will pray for us now and in the future as we, its people, try to live up to the ideals of St Chad.

LEFT: *Lichfield Cathedral from the south-east.*

The story of Lichfield Cathedral begins with a name and a legend. The name is Chad, the legend that a thousand Christians were martyred here around AD 300, during the reign of the Roman emperor Diocletian, and that Lichfield means 'field or place of the dead'. If it was already a martyr shrine, this may explain why, as Bede the 8th-century church historian tells us, 'Chad established his episcopal seat in the town of *Lyccidfelth* [Lichfield]. There he built himself a house near the church [of St Mary], where he used to retire privately with seven or eight brethren in order to pray or study whenever his work and preaching permitted.'

Chad was a remarkable man. Formerly a pupil of St Aidan at Lindisfarne, he was appointed Bishop of Mercia in 669, moving the focus of the diocese from Repton to Lichfield. The Christian Church was weak there at that time and Chad, although bishop for only three years, brought many to the Christian faith. Stories tell of a humble, zealous man of transparent godliness. Bede records that he died in 672 and was first buried 'close by Saint Mary's Church', where miracles were said to have taken place, and that later his body was transferred to a new church, dedicated to St Peter, which was built nearby.

It is thought that these two Saxon churches stood on the site of the present cathedral, on an east-west axis in line with the holy well, still found by St Chad's church, on the far side of Stowe Pool. In this well, Chad is reputed to have baptized converts, and stood to pray! Thus Lichfield became the centre for the cult of St Chad and a place of pilgrimage.

ABOVE: One of a series of Kempe windows from the Chapter House, showing St Aidan teaching boys at Lindisfarne, including St Chad. ⑦

LEFT: The Carpet Page from the cathedral's greatest treasure, the 8th-century Lichfield Gospels, an illuminated Latin manuscript of Matthew, Mark and part of Luke, on show in the Chapter House. Such pages, bearing a cross, are a common feature of gospel manuscripts in the Lindisfarne tradition. ⑦

ABOVE: A tile roundel from the presbytery floor. Archbishop Theodore orders Chad to ride a horse around the Diocese of Mercia. ⑨

The building of the Norman cathedral at the end of the 11th century marked the next major advance in Lichfield's Christian life. Although the see had moved first to Chester in 1075 and then to Coventry in 1102, a new stone cathedral was begun in 1085. Roger de Clinton (Bishop 1129–48) was strongly associated with its later development, and building work continued over the next 200 years. As well as appointing a dean and prebendaries to the cathedral, de Clinton fortified the Close and laid out the city of Lichfield. His memory is perpetuated in the arms of the cathedral and diocese, the arms borne by him in the Second Crusade, in which he died.

It was once thought that little, if any, of the Norman cathedral remained, but Sir George Gilbert Scott's restoration work of the 1850s uncovered its foundations in the choir, and recent archaeological work has increased our knowledge considerably. Norman stonework was found in both choir aisles, and can be seen in the wall linking the south choir aisle to St Chad's Head Chapel. Although the dimensions are not fully known, the Norman building is likely to have been similar in style and size to Buildwas Abbey, built by de Clinton near Much Wenlock in Shropshire.

The choir ended in an apse, which presumably held the shrine of St Chad, and was flanked by two smaller apses. In due course, a square-ended chapel was added to the central apse. Then, both apse and chapel were replaced by a larger square-ended choir, providing more room for pilgrimage to the shrine.

Towards the end of the 12th century, work began on replacing the Norman cathedral with a more magnificent building, built in the latest Gothic style. This is, broadly speaking, the one we see today.

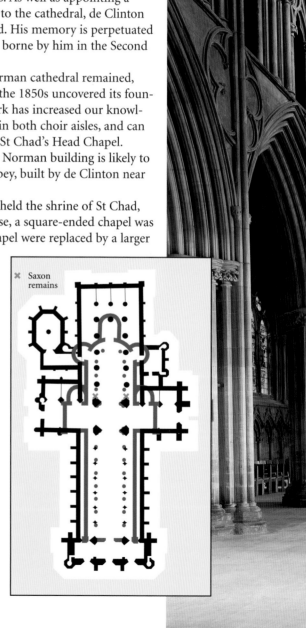

✖ Saxon remains

ABOVE: *One of the Norman stones found in the foundations and walls during the Victorian restoration of the cathedral and now in the Visitors' Centre. The Green Man is a common motif of the period.*

RIGHT: *Previous shapes: in red, the likely ground plan of the Norman cathedral, showing the location of Saxon remains discovered in the 1990s; superimposed in black is the plan of the cathedral as it was in 1300, before the addition of the Lady Chapel.*

OPPOSITE: *The nave looking east. The perfectly proportioned Geometric Gothic style carries the eye down to Scott's screen and the 16th-century Herckenrode glass of the Lady Chapel beyond.* ①

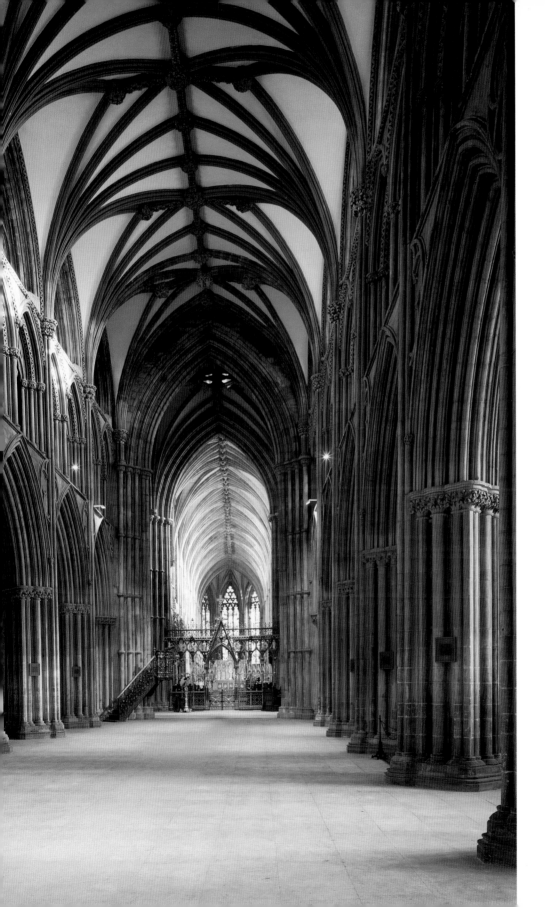

L ichfield's Gothic cathedral has had one of the most interesting histories of any in England, surviving the destructive force of the Reformation and three Civil War sieges, and undergoing three major restorations before the 20th century.

The building was planned by Hugh de Nonant (Bishop 1188–98), who structured its life by writing the first set of statutes of any English cathedral. It demonstrates all the major styles of Gothic architecture.

The western bays of the choir, begun in 1200, include Norman Transitional decoration on some pillars. The blind arcading and the small, pointed windows show the simple elegance of Early English Gothic. The arcading of the transepts (south 1220, north 1240) is also Early English, as is the north window (restored in the 19th century) but the great south window is in the later Perpendicular style.

ABOVE: Statues of saints on the west front. Left to right: James, Stephen and Clement.

Before the Norman nave was replaced, important building took place to the north and south of the choir. On the north side, a vestibule, with pedilavium, leads into the Chapter House (1249), in which the Chapters of Lichfield and Coventry met to elect their bishop. Octagonal in shape, it is both unusual and beautiful. Its windows depict the life of St Chad and medieval carvings include Adam and Eve on the east wall and a cat with a mouse over the bishop's seat.

The library above the Chapter House contains one of the cathedral's most memorable features: a late 13th-century tiled pavement, imitated by Minton's when they tiled the choir in the 1850s during Scott's restoration.

To the south of the choir is St Chad's Head Chapel. Here were kept the skull of the saint and an arm bone in a casket. Pilgrims would have mounted a staircase, walked around the head, and then down a second staircase, which still exists in the wall. The pressure of pilgrimage is thought to have led the Chapter to close one staircase and build, instead, a balcony, from which the precious relic could be shown to the passing crowd below.

Lichfield's nave was completed in 1285 in Geometric Gothic style. It is said to be one of the finest in the country, with excellent proportions, angular decoration and remarkable clerestory windows.

ABOVE: A verger shows how the skull of St Chad was shown to pilgrims from the St Chad's Head Chapel. ⑯

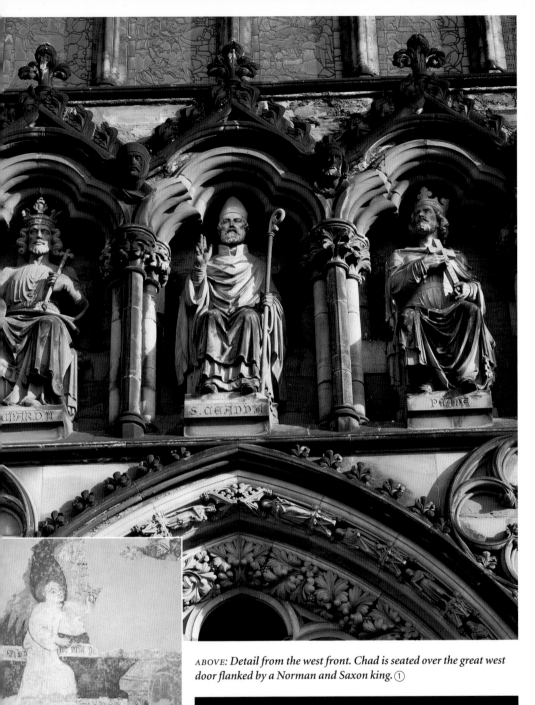

ABOVE: *Detail from the west front. Chad is seated over the great west door flanked by a Norman and Saxon king.* ①

ABOVE: *Detail of an angel from a medieval wall painting of the Trinity, marking Bishop de Langton's chantry chapel in the south choir aisle.* ⑮

THE MYSTERIOUS BEND

The strange bend in the cathedral (a feature shared with a number of medieval cathedrals) is attributed by some to a curve in the bedrock. Dr Plot, in the 18th century, ingeniously saw it as a readjustment to the east-west line following the invention of the compass. Most authorities think it results from the building of the Lady Chapel.

The Lady Chapel was begun in the time of Walter de Langton (Bishop 1296–1321), and completed in about 1330. Built in the Decorated style, with yet another style of blind arcading, the nodding ogee, it provided a fine setting for a new shrine of St Chad. This cost £2,000 and took the form of a small church, decorated with colourful statues and adorned with precious gifts and jewels.

It was said by some that when the chapel was built, and the east end wall demolished to incorporate the addition, its walls did not match in size and that William Ramsey, the king's architect, solved the problem by knocking down the eastern bays of the choir and rebuilding them on a curve. A less romantic explanation would be that because of the plague or lack of money, the rebuilding of the choir, in the Decorated style, was never completed.

By St Chad's Head Chapel, the transition can be seen: one pillar combines two styles of decoration, the blind arcading becomes more ornate and the vaulting also changes.

By 1400, the cathedral looked very different from the way it appears today. Pilgrims approaching the west front would have seen the original array of 113 statues there, most of which were painted and some gilded, as were the statues in the choir and Lady Chapel. Today almost all of these are Victorian reproductions. Some medieval painting can still be seen in the canopies of the Lady Chapel.

Inside, the cathedral was much darker, not just because of the dense medieval glass but also the painted stonework, which can still be seen in the Chapter House and in the arcading of the choir aisles. The roof vaulting was also painted, though the present decoration dates mainly from 1988.

There were some 15 altars and chapels, at each of which chantry priests said Mass daily for the souls of the departed. Today, piscinas and aumbreys still mark their position.

The medieval cathedral was, then, a colourful and busy place, as the throng of pilgrims, particularly on St Chad's Day, 2 March, visited his shrine for prayer and chantry priests said Mass at the many altars. All this was to change at the Reformation.

ABOVE: *Madonna and Child, a detail from a window above the Lady Chapel altar.* ⑫

BELOW: *A cat with a mouse in the arcade sculptures of the medieval Chapter House.* ⑦

LEFT: *The Lady Chapel has the magnificent Herckenrode glass, brought to Lichfield in 1803; the 19th-century replacement statues of women saints; a reredos, the figures of which were carved in Oberammergau; and the Selwyn memorial. The shrine of St Chad is a focus for prayer.* ⑪

9

In the 16th century Henry VIII led the Church in England to a break with Rome, with great implications for the practice of the Faith. The elaborate medieval worship with its emphasis on masses for the dead disappeared, chantry chapels were disendowed and the shrine of Chad was taken away. Stone altars were destroyed, and ornaments and relics dispersed. The bright walls were whitewashed, statues destroyed and monuments broken. Pilgrimage came to an end and the cathedral took on a very austere appearance.

Lichfield Cathedral suffered more than any other cathedral during the Civil War. At first a Royalist stronghold, the Close was taken by Parliamentary forces in 1643, recaptured a month later and then taken again in 1646. Cannonfire holed the roof and destroyed the central spire. On top of this, Cromwell's troops, once in possession, destroyed statues and monuments, defaced the carvings and caused other extensive damage.

In the years following the Civil War, Lichfield's clergy were made to suffer greatly for their erstwhile allegiance to monarchy and Church. Cromwell's Puritans, under Presbyterian influence from Scotland, were against bishops and against the Prayer Book, the symbol of the new Church of England. Both were thrown out as the Church became more Protestant. In 1660 the restoration of Charles II brought new hope. Precentor Higgins and the reformed Chapter began the long process of restoration. Regular worship began in the Chapter House, one of the least damaged parts of the building. John Hacket (Bishop 1661–70) oversaw the rebuilding of the cathedral, but gone for ever was its

medieval ornamentation. Light from the plain glass windows would have shown up the defaced carvings of the arcading, still visible today. The whitewashed walls were broken only by the niches where statues had been torn away. The fine Gothic screen, separating the choir from the Lady Chapel, had been covered to hide its mutilation by a Classical-style screen, based on one in the Chapel Royal at Whitehall; damaged monuments were everywhere. Old chapels were put to new, more mundane uses as vestries and consistory courts.

ABOVE: *Cannonballs and fragments of grenades from the Civil War sieges were found in the Close and are now in the Visitors' Centre.*

RIGHT: *A chalice, one item of the silverware commissioned by Bishop Hacket to replace that lost during the Civil War, is on show in the Treasury, with the Lang Lichfield silver collection.* ⑯

Serve God and be chearefull

Giving thanks to God, for the pious example of Bishop Hacket, by which after generations of benefactors have been moved to carry on his work, towards the complete reparation of this Cathedral Church, a grateful diocese dedicates this window to his honoured memory on the Festival of S. Chad, a.d. 1901.

ABOVE: *A 19th-century window, by C.E. Kempe in the south choir aisle, showing Bishop Hacket setting about the restoration of the cathedral after the Civil War.* ⑮

Although Lichfield's cathedral changed little until the 1790s, by contrast the 18th century was a very lively period in the history of the city.

Erasmus Darwin (1731–1802), grandfather of Charles Darwin (of evolution fame), was a radical, inventive scientist and physician who contributed to the Industrial Revolution locally, and greatly influenced England's intellectual life, through the Lunar Society.

Although living near the cathedral, Darwin was an agnostic and critical of the Church – a true disciple of the Age of Reason. His house, facing Beacon Street, is owned by the Chapter, and is now the Erasmus Darwin Centre.

Samuel Johnson (1709–84), by contrast, was a staunch churchman, worshipping regularly in St Mary's Church. Born in Breadmarket Street, he was educated locally, eventually going to London with David Garrick, the actor, to achieve fame as a writer and compiler of his great English dictionary.

In the cathedral, the repairs of the 1660s were beginning to need attention. The 15th-century library to the north of the nave, in a dangerous state, was taken down and its books, given by the Duchess of Somerset in 1673, moved to a room above the Chapter House. The west front statues were also dangerous, and all but three of them were removed. They were replaced by one row of kings, whose weathered medieval stone was finished in Roman cement.

ABOVE: *A corner of the 15th-century Vicars' Close, with houses originally built for the singing men of the cathedral.*

LEFT: *The cathedral from the east, reflected in the Stowe Pool.*

ABOVE: An 1819 engraving by Britton, showing the cathedral from the south-east.

The weight of the nave roof was causing the walls to lean outwards, as they still do. James Wyatt saved them from collapsing by removing 500 tons of stone from the vaulting. He also carried out extensive work in the south transept, Lady Chapel and, notably, in the choir which the Dean and Chapter considered too cold and too small for worship. Wyatt's solution was to create a church within the cathedral. He filled in the arches of the choir, and placed a full stone screen at the west end of the choir, on which he put the organ with a glass screen up to the vaulting. Removing the high altar, he then erected seating right through to the Lady Chapel area. By 1800, the cathedral once again looked very different, but this was not to last long.

ABOVE RIGHT: A roundel in the south choir aisle commemorating Erasmus Darwin, physician, scientist, inventor and polymath, the grandfather of Charles. His life and work is explored in the Erasmus Darwin Centre in Beacon Street. ⑰

RIGHT: A bust commemorating Samuel Johnson, the 18th-century writer and lexicographer, who was born in Lichfield's Breadmarket Street. ⑱

In the early part of the 19th century, little significant structural work was done, but the cathedral purchased the beautiful 16th-century Herckenrode glass from Brooke Boothby, and installed it in the Lady Chapel. Sir Francis Chantrey added another great treasure when he was commissioned to make the monument to the 'Sleeping Children', now a focal point in the south choir aisle.

Then, in the 1850s, the Dean and Chapter began a restoration of the cathedral which was to continue until the end of the century.

Sir George Gilbert Scott was first commissioned to undertake the restoration of the choir. The changes wrought were dramatic. Scott began by reversing Wyatt's work, unblocking the arches of the choir, restoring the high altar and, once again, creating a separate Lady Chapel. His work showed immense sensitivity.

Gothic style was again in fashion, and where possible Scott retained the original medieval work; where he could not, he imitated it. Thus the unique join of the Early English and Decorated architecture of the choir was retained, and defaced sculptures stood side by side with new carving in the same style. Similarly, on walls and pillars, 19th-century reproductions accompanied Norman Transitional and Gothic decorations.

Wyatt's stone screen was replaced with a fine metal one by Skidmore. New Jacobean-style choir stalls, executed along with the pulpit

ABOVE: *The screen made by Skidmore was installed during Scott's restoration of the 1850s.* ②

and aisle gates by Evans, matched the bishop's throne. From fragments of medieval tiles found during the work, Minton's created a remarkable tile pavement from screen to altar.

Over the next 40 years, Scott was asked to continue his work throughout the building. The whitewash on walls was removed to reveal traces of the medieval paintwork, statues were replaced in the Lady Chapel and choir, and in the 1880s the poor Roman cement statues on the west front were removed and the façade restored to its medieval splendour.

One of the last places restored was St Chad's Head Chapel. The vaulting was replaced and the bosses carved with scenes from the life of St Chad. Once again medieval features, like the Early English windows and two fine carvings of the Green Man, were retained. By 1900 the cathedral had been renewed, within and without.

LEFT: *A Victorian window by C.E. Kempe depicting the healing of the lame man at the Beautiful Gate (Acts 3: 1–10).* ⑭

RIGHT: *Detail from the 19th-century Minton tiles of the presbytery.* ⑨

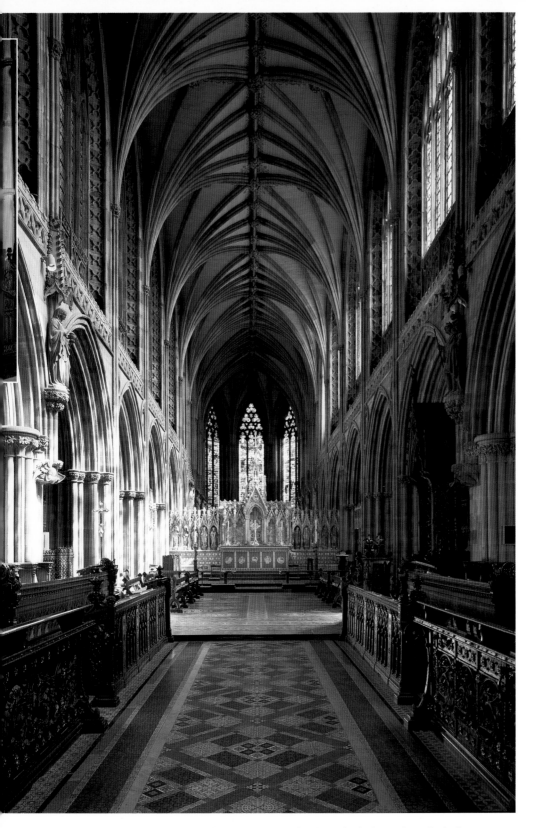

ABOVE: *The choir and presbytery, with the high altar and, right, the Bishop's throne (or cathedra).* ⑧

The great work of restoration and preservation continued into the 20th century and down to the present day. Modern developments show the same attention to detail as in other times.

In the sanctuary, statues were placed in the niches behind the high altar in 1902. Later, Scott's imaginative work in the sedilia to the south of the altar was matched by new work to the north. In 1907, the organ was moved from St Stephen's Chapel to its present position high up above the north choir aisle. It was restored in 1974 and again in 2000, when a nave extension console was added.

A 750th-anniversary appeal in 1946 allowed work to take place on the buttresses of the north nave wall, and the paving of the Close. In 1957 nearly £250,000 was raised, the central spire rebuilt and the roofing considerably improved. The south transept and buttresses once again received attention. Inside, St Michael's Chapel was redesigned as the military chapel of the Staffordshire Regiment.

In the 1980s the three medieval wall paintings were restored and, following another appeal, a 10-year repair programme launched. Subsequent work on the vaulting, towers, spires and roof space has enhanced the cathedral's beauty and increased its ability to continue the work of God. With new work on the lighting and sound, the cathedral is fit for the worship of God, for music and drama, and to receive pilgrims and visitors into the 21st century.

ABOVE: The Book of Remembrance located in St Michael's Chapel, where the campaigns of the Staffordshire Regiments are commemorated. (18)

A Christian community gathered here 1,300 years ago and has served God and His people ever since. Through the years this religious activity has changed in emphasis and changes have resulted in the building and its furnishings. The present cathedral is an intriguing record of the changing life of this Christian community.

For the many visitors who need interpretation of this record, the Visitors' Centre offers a welcome, hospitality and information.

With a bookshop and tearoom nearby and the increasing use of the cathedral for the performance of great music and large diocesan and county services, Lichfield Cathedral continues to worship God, support the faithful and serve the people, as it ever has.

ABOVE: *The magnificent tiled pavement, part of Scott's restoration, stretching from the screen to the high altar. The tile designs were based on fragments found under the floor in the 1850s, and are similar to those in the library.* ⑨

RIGHT: *The kneeling figure of Henry Ryder (Bishop 1824–36), by Sir Francis Chantrey.* ④

LEFT: *Detail from the Minton tiles in the choir.* ⑧

The treasures of Lichfield Cathedral span the centuries, from the 8th-century Lichfield Gospels to the Lang Lichfield Silver Collection, commissioned in 1991. The Gospel manuscript (see p.2) is on show in the Chapter House, where all the major illustrated pages are reproduced. Also in the Chapter House is the medieval wall painting of the *Assumption of Our Lady*, one of three paintings dating from around 1400, the other two being in the south choir aisle. The most important stained glass is the Herckenrode glass, dating from the 1530s, which, with other Flemish glass, is in the Lady Chapel. Most of Lichfield's glass dates from the later 19th century, and includes a large number of Kempe windows and some fine glass by Betton & Evans (1819). Amongst several monuments, a few medieval but most *c.*19th-century, the Sleeping Children and that of Bishop Ryder by Sir Francis Chantrey are outstanding. A fine bust of Bishop Woods by Sir Jacob Epstein stands in the vestibule.

The most notable reminders of Sir George Gilbert Scott's extensive 19th-century restoration are the metal screen connecting the choir to the nave, and the splendid Minton pavement of the choir, with designs based on those of the 13th century. These medieval patterns are still to be found on the library floor. Finally, in the Consistory Court, there is the fine silver collection which is in regular use for services and which sits alongside the impressive silverware commissioned by Bishop Hacket after the Civil War.

ABOVE: The Chad Loving Cup, made by Kevin Coates as part of the 1991 Lang Lichfield Silver Commission, is on show in the Treasury/Consistory Court, and is used during the commemoration of St Chad on 2 March. ⑯

ABOVE: Modern embroidery depicting the prebends of the cathedral adorn the Jacobean-style, 19th-century choir stalls by George Evans, uncle of the novelist George Eliot. ⑧

ABOVE: **The Sleeping Children,** *two young sisters, Ellen-Jane and Marianne, who died in 1812, sensitively portrayed by Sir Francis Chantrey in 1817. Chantrey also carved the figure of Bishop Ryder in the north transept.* ⑭

LEFT: *The monument commemorating Bishop Selwyn, first Bishop of New Zealand and Bishop of Lichfield 1867–78. The tiles show his work among the Maoris and in the industry of Staffordshire.* ⑬

RIGHT: *A bust of Edward Woods (Bishop 1937–53), by Sir Jacob Epstein, which stands in the vestibule. The vestibule, leading to the Chapter House, contains a medieval pedilavium, used for the foot-washing ceremony on Maundy Thursday.* ⑥

EDWARD SYDNEY WOODS
BISHOP OF LICHFIELD 1937-1953

The Cathedral Close has its own story to tell. In medieval times a stone wall surrounded it on four sides, whilst the south was additionally protected by the Moggs, now Minster Pool. Evidence of the fortifications can still be seen in the south-east corner, where the wall and the foundations of the south gate have been uncovered. In the north-east corner the remains of Bishop de Clinton's palace are evident. Vicars' Close, to the west, retains its 15th-century form, and several other houses were rebuilt round medieval remains. The Bishop's Palace, now the School, built in 1687, was enlarged by Bishop Selwyn in 1867. The Deanery, which is next to it, is early 18th-century.

On the south side, St Mary's House in the corner is built round a medieval dwelling and still incorporates some of the wall and a staircase tower from the 14th century. Opposite this, the Visitors' Centre uses the restored Muniment Room, once a stable block for Bishop Hacket. Newton's College to the south-west, the gift of John Newton in 1806, leads the visitor out through the site of the old Westgate and into Beacon Street and the city.

The ancient city still bears the marks of Bishop de Clinton, who laid it out on a grid pattern in the 13th century. To the south is St John's Hospital, once a hospice for pilgrims visiting the cathedral. Walk from here into the city and you pass the site of the friary, suppressed in 1538.

In the Market Place, Johnson's birthplace stands next to St Mary's Church, now the Heritage Centre, exhibiting much of the city's colourful history. Walking eastwards, past St Michael's Church, you come to St Chad's Church, built on the site of the ancient well used by St Chad in the 7th century. From here you can see, across the Stowe Pool, the three spires of the cathedral pointing to Heaven, but the earthly focus of 1,300 years of Christian history.